GW01168089

Printed in Great Britain
by Amazon

76038136R00068